The Many Fears of Miela ...the Cat

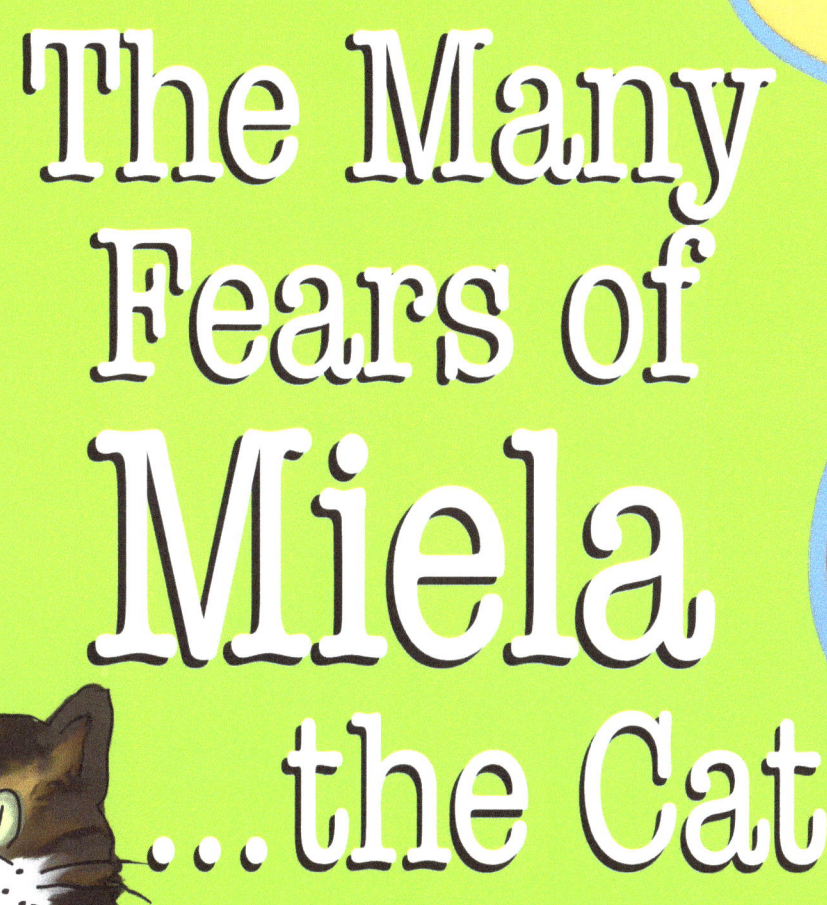

By: Patrice Maguire
Illustrations by: Eric Pipes

The Many Fears of Miela the Cat
Copyright © 2018—Patrice Maguire
ALL RIGHTS RESERVED UNDER U.S., PAN-AMERICAN AND INTERNATIONAL COPYRIGHTS.
No part of this publication may be reproduced, stored in a retrieval system or transmitted in any form by mechanical, electronic, photocopying, recording or otherwise without the prior written consent of the author.

Published by:

Little Oaks Publishing
18896 Greenwell Springs Road
Greenwell Springs, LA 70739
www.thepublishedword.com

ISBN: 978-1-940461-76-2 Trade version
       978-1-940461-78-6 Casebound version

Printed on demand in the U.S., the U.K. and Australia
For Worldwide Distribution

This is a real story about a real cat with real fears like yours and mine.

Once upon a time, there was a little cat named Miela.

She was a very pretty cat.

She had a black spot on the tip of her little pink nose.

Her fur was many different colors, and her eyes were a beautiful shade of green.

She was small, but she never let that stop her. Miela had many fears, but she had to learn to get past her fears so that she could survive.

Miela had a rough start in life. Her people family abandoned her when she was still a kitten. They didn't want her anymore, so they put her in their car and drove her to the woods and left her there.

The car ride there was frightening. Miela had never been in a car before. Now she never wanted to be in one again because it took her to a scary place.

It was never clear to Miela why her family didn't want her. Her heart was broken, and she wondered if she had done something wrong.

Feeling unwanted and unloved was probably the worst feeling in the whole world. Now she was alone in a strange place, with no food or water, and she was very sad and afraid.

When it got dark, there were a lot of strange noises that Miela had never heard before. Those noises made her even more afraid. She would hide under bushes at night and keep watch for any danger that might be around her, such as hungry wild animals. Every little sound startled her.

Since she had to stay awake all night, she was very tired by morning. She would take naps during the day. But even during the day, there were things to fear— such as snakes, hawks and spiders. Miela always had to be on her guard.

After napping, Miela would carefully walk around looking for food and water. When it rained, there were puddles of water she could drink from. And sometimes she would catch a small mouse to eat.

But that wasn't every day, so some days she was very hungry and thirsty. And she was always tired. She had to stay in the woods because there were big hawks flying around outside of the woods looking for small animals to eat. Miela was always surrounded by danger.

One day Miela noticed two boys walking on the road close to the woods. One boy was taller than the other one. The taller boy had blonde hair, and the other boy had brown hair. She noticed them walking almost every day for about a week. Thinking they might be nice boys, she decided to be brave and let them see her as they walked by.

The boys started walking toward Miela and talking to her in a friendly tone of voice, but she got scared and ran away. She remembered how her people family had treated her in the past and thought maybe the boys would try to hurt her too.

The next day the boys walked to where they had seen Miela the day before. She saw that the boys had something in their hands. One of the boys was carrying a clear bag filled with small brown morsels of something. And the other boy was carrying a bottle filled with a clear liquid in one hand and a small bowl in his other.

Miela thought maybe it was food and water. It had been over a day since she had eaten. Being so hungry and thirsty, she decided to take a chance and trust the boys.

When they saw her, they poured some food in a pile on the ground and poured the water in the bowl beside the food. They didn't want to frighten Miela again, so they slowly walked away and watched her from a distance.

Miela, thinking it was now safe to eat and drink, carefully crept over to the food and ate until her little belly was full.

It felt so good to be full. This made Miela very happy. She started to think that maybe some people could be trusted. The boys brought Miela food and water every day, and every day she looked forward to her delicious meal.

One day Miela could sense that a very bad storm was coming. She knew that hiding under a bush wasn't going to be enough to keep her dry. She needed to find a better place to take shelter. She searched and searched until she found the perfect place. It was a hollowed-out dead tree that had fallen over. She felt safe inside of it.

The storm came. The rain poured from the sky. Miela had never seen so much rain. The wind howled angrily. It tore leaves and branches from the trees as it blew. Miela was very afraid. She didn't like the loud noises. The storm lasted two whole days and nights. Miela was safe and sound in her new hiding place. She liked it so much that she decided to make it her new home.

Once the storm was over, Miela was very hungry, so she decided to go looking for the two boys. She could not find them where she used to meet them every day. She went back the next day and the day after that, but they were

not there. So she went back to hunting mice, but they were even harder to find since the storm, and Miela was getting weak with hunger.

Miela knew she had to do something to survive. She decided she would take a long journey to look for the two boys. She missed them and hoped that they missed her too.

"But maybe they didn't miss her," she thought.

"Maybe they had abandoned her like her people family had. Maybe they didn't like her after all."

"Maybe something bad had happened to them during the storm."

She had to find out for herself. So she found the courage to search for the truth, and she hoped this journey would have a good ending.

Remembering the direction the boys had walked from, Miela left early the next morning to look for them. She walked slowly through the woods that day, being very careful not to become food for a wild animal.

She took naps under bushes here and there along the way when she got very tired. She became more and more hungry with every step.

Late that evening, Miela heard two familiar voices and laughs. It sounded like the two boys! She became very excited! She would have to step out of the woods and into danger of becoming prey to a hawk to get to them. But she

felt very desperate, so she knew she had to try.

She crept very cautiously along the fence line in the direction of the voices. As she walked, the voices got louder and louder, until she knew she had finally found them.

Miela found a low area under the fence that was between her and the boys and then crawled under it. Now she was in their backyard. And there they were. She could see them! She meowed loudly twice, and they heard her.

They were so happy to see her, and it made her happy that they were happy. The boys did miss her and liked her after all.

They ran inside their house and came back outside with food and water. She ate until she couldn't eat another bite. When Miela was finished, she left the yard to hide in the nearby woods again. She wasn't sure if it was safe to stay in the backyard or even if the boys wanted her to stay.

Miela visited the boys every day until she started trusting them more and more. The boys had a mom and dad, an older brother and a dog named Mr. Bear. Over time she learned to trust them as well. She would even let them pet her sometimes.

One day she felt so safe and secure there with them that she didn't want to leave anymore, so she didn't. She wanted their home to be her home, and they wanted the same thing.

Miela loved her new home and her new people family. Her new family loved her very much as well and took very good care of her. To show that Miela was now a member of their family, they bought her a pretty new collar with a little bell on it and a soft warm place to sleep.

She was finally safe, secure, wanted and loved. It was the best feeling in the whole world.

The End.

Considering Miela's Fears

As you can see, Miela had many fears. She was afraid of being alone, afraid of being hurt by people, afraid of stormy weather, afraid of rejection, afraid of the dark, and afraid of wild animals that could hurt her. Maybe her biggest fear was being stuck in her fear and never experiencing a good life or knowing how it felt to be truly loved or part of a happy family. But even though she had reasons to fear, she never let her fears stop her. Her hopes were bigger than her fears.

Are you sometimes afraid of the same things Miela was afraid of? Are you afraid of being alone, afraid of being hurt by people, afraid of bad weather, or afraid of the dark? Maybe you don't have wild animals hunting you but maybe you have a bully at school or in your neighborhood who is mean to you. Maybe you heard something on the television or the radio that frightened you. Your fears may not go away, but you can still be brave and courageous like Miela. God will help you if you ask Him. The Bible says, in 1 John 4:18, that perfect love drives out fear.

When you truly understand how much God loves you and that you can trust Him, you will be able to do His will despite your fears.

First, list your fears with the date on the following page. Maybe your mom and dad can help you. Then, when God answers your prayers, write down how He helped you with the date on the page titled Answers to Prayers. This way you can keep track of all the ways God is faithful to answer your prayers and it will cause your faith and courage to grow.

Now let's pray:

Dear God,

Sometimes I am afraid of _____ (this is where you name the fears that you wrote on your list). Help me to remember that You love me and are always with me. Help me to know that I can trust You. Make me brave and courageous like Miela. Help me to get past my fears and live the best life that You have for me. I ask these things in Your Son Jesus' name. Thank You God. Amen!

List of Fears

Answers to Prayers

    Miela came into our lives during the summer of 2012. We had just moved to Baton Rouge, Louisiana that June. The storm that Miela went through was Hurricane Isaac.

    We feel very blessed to have Miela as part of our family. She brings us much joy, and we are thankful for her.

    I hope you have enjoyed her story and have been inspired to move past your fears and live your best life.

Patrice Maguire

If you enjoyed this Little Oaks book by Patrice Maguire, look for:

The Wonderful Life of Mr. Bear

www.ingramcontent.com/pod-product-compliance
Lightning Source LLC
LaVergne TN
LVHW070837080426
835510LV00026B/3422